ANTHOLOGY OF POETRY
BY
YOUNG AMERICANS®

1998 EDITION
VOLUME LXXXVI

Published by Anthology of Poetry, Inc.

©*Anthology of Poetry by Young Americans*®
1998 Edition
Volume LXXXVI

All Rights Reserved©

Printed in the United States of America

To submit poems
for consideration in the 1999 edition of the
Anthology of Poetry by Young Americans®,
send to:
> Anthology of Poetry, Inc.
> PO Box 698
> Asheboro, NC 27204-0698

Authors responsible
for originality of poems submitted.

The Anthology of Poetry, Inc.
307 East Salisbury • P.O. Box 698
Asheboro, NC   27204-0698

ISBN: 1-883931-13-4

Anthology of Poetry by Young Americans®
is a registered trademark of
Anthology of Poetry, Inc.

The poetry in the 1998 edition of the *Anthology of Poetry by Young Americans®* continues our nine year tradition of publishing a diverse and eclectic volume of children's poetry. Our poets come from all over the United States, from children in kindergarten to seniors in high school. They come from all the different social, economic, religious and philosophical backgrounds possible, but they all share with us a snapshot of some part of their lives or thoughts. The works of art represented here give us a picture of our children only possible with the vivid and colorful language of poetry We tried to present the poems as the author wrote them, in their format and punctuation.

In response to the numerous requests we received to dedicate this years anthology to the "Year of the Ocean", we have covered the volume in a deep blue. We would like to extend a special thanks to all the poets who participated. We are expecting great things from them in the future.

The Editors

TEARS

Tears rolling down my face
Because I'm missing you
Why did you have to go
and leave me so empty and cold
I wish I could see you for one brief second
just to say I love you
I know you don't want me to be like this
but it's the fact, I never said good-bye
I was there with you, you getting better
So then I left without a good-bye
without knowing that would be the last time
I would see your glowing face
I need you now to help me
through this rough time of adolescent life
to hold me near and say I'll be all right
I miss the way we laughed and cried
little things I hold so dear
Even though I was young
I still remember it quite clearly
and every time I think of you
it brings a tear to my eye
So here I am sitting here
writing this poem
just to say I love you
and need you near

Tracy Sluka
Age: 15

BOBBING FOR APPLES

B obbing for apples
O h, you got one
B ob for another one
B obbing is so fun!
I n the water I found
N othing but apples so round
G o bobbing for apples it's a lot of fun!

Brian E. Leenheer
Age: 9

THERE WAS A HALLOWEEN CAT

He wore a black mask,
He looked like a bat.
He got a lot of treats,
Then he shared with his mouse.

Nicholas Balazs
Age: 8

NIGHT CREATURE

B lack as the darkest night.
A ctive when the night comes
T errifying to see on a pitch-black night.

Robert Hodermarsky
Age: 8

A FUNNY SCHOOL DAY

One day I got up for school,
The weather outside was cool.
I put on the cat,
Instead of my hat.
And I really felt like a fool.

Ryan Giffin

TURKEY SOUP

A little of this,
A little of that,
A big fat turkey,
And Abe Lincoln's hat.
Some spices,
Some carrots,
Some lemon meringue,
Turkey feathers,
A gunshot that went BANG!
Some beans,
Some lettuce,
Some corn on the cob,
My homework,
It looks like a slob!
I know this sounds strange
But it's true, it's true!
I hate it so much
I do! I do!
Some apple pie
I think I'm going to die!
I do! I do!
Bye Bye

Briana Marie Hurt
Age: 9

EARTH'S SEASONS

Spring is just beginning
and the birds are now all singing
and we all are having fun,
bathing in the summer sun.
Soon all our trees
have lost their leaves
and we are bundled up
in our winter coats
catching leaves
by jumping up and up.
As they fall
I start to dance
and my cat and dog automatically prance.
My cat is in my house,
trying to grab a mouse
which is scurrying on by
with its winter supply.
Soon it will be winter
and the frost will pierce my cheeks.
If only it was spring again
but, oh, the basement leaks!
So, no, just think again,
let the next season come
with the previous one's end.

Karen Dernar
Age: 10

THE WITCH

W ake up it's Halloween
I t's time to trick-or-treat
T he children are having fun
C hildren like Halloween
H appy Halloween everybody

Alexandra Giuliani
Age: 9

SCHOOL IS OVER

SCHOOL is over school is done
Now it's time to start the fun
Since it's summer here and there
Let's relax and sit on a chair
While the music is playing nice
We will see grass but not snow and ice
While we are in the pool
I am so glad I am not in school
When the leaves grow back in place
I will put on my happy face
If I stayed in school one more day
I would never get to play
I hope time won't fly
I do not want summer to say bye, bye.

Peter Haftkowyez
Age: 9

BILL'S BAD DAY

There once was a man named Bill
Who one day became very ill
He went to his bed
But bumped his head instead
And took a Tylenol pill

Bill couldn't sleep that night
He was having a terrible fright
Of falling right down
With his face in a frown
He fell off his bed at the sight

He woke up the very next day
And went in the yard to play
He fell on his knee
The blood he did see
And said "What more could happen to me?"

Brian Green
Age: 11

There once was a dragon from Snave,
Who hid for ten years in a cave.
One day he came out,
And was slaughtered no doubt,
Because he was not brave.

Julie M. Hritz
Age: 11

TWIRLING TWISTER

Twister, twister in the sky,
You spin so fast I could die.
When I heard something loud,
I turned around and saw the cloud.
I saw my brother in the sky,
Then he hit me in the eye.
I went tumbling down the street,
And stumbled to my feet.
Then it came to suck me in,
But, I jumped into a trash bin!

Vince Urbanski
Age: 11

WINTER MORNING

Quiet wind, a gleam of light,
still trees in the forest glen.
As the tiny snowflake fairies,
blanket the meadow of life.
While the birds fly above,
to the promised south.
And the little flowers hide,
from the sprinkling snow.
One chilly and restless,
winter morning.

Lindsay Elizabeth Jackson
Age: 12

I REFUSED

I refused to go to school today.
I refused to ride the bus.
I refused to receive all that homework.
Oh, all that horrible homework!
I refused to take all that torture.

I refused to go to school today.
I refused to sit there all day long.
I refused to stare at the chalkboard.
I refused to do my arithmetic.
I refused to know just why.

Jason M. Baker
Age: 11

A MONSTER UNDER MY BED

M onster sound from a monster.
O nly out loud the squeaky sound.
U nder my bed I hear it at night.
S omeone or something under my bed,
    the squeak gets louder in my head.
E nds and starts under my bed then
    it said, "Trick-or-treat, could you
    get me some cheese to eat?"

Vince Schuck
Age: 9

IT'S NOT A CINCH TO PINCH

There once was a man on the beach
He fought a big giant peach
Out came a crab
His nose it did nab
And out of his mouth came a screech

He pulled the crab off of his nose
It was as red as a rose
He threw the crab out to sea
With all of his possible glee
He struck a victorious pose

The man walked down the beach
His house he was trying to reach
The crab washed ashore
And pinched him some more
Once more he let out a screech

He kicked the crab onto his house
And called it a dirty red louse
The crab walked away
With nothing to say
As quiet as a small mouse

Ted Bienias
Age: 11

DINO-DAY

I wake up and I hear a roar
I get out of bed and open the door
And what's there but a dinosaur!

I sit down and I eat my lunch
A green claw grabs my carrot and crunch
And what's left but a dinosaur!

I lie down and I go to sleep
I hear the sound of reptile feet
You guessed it: it's a dinosaur!

Roland Rovito
Age: 9

SCHOOL

School is fun, we learn every day.
We come to learn not to play.
Reading is my specialty. What is yours?
In the books animals even roar!
ISLAND OF THE BLUE DOLPHINS,
and RAMONA THE PEST,
Those are the books that I love best.
Beverly Cleary and Scott O'Dell,
"Oops! I have to go, there's the bell!"

Allison Kay
Age: 10

WONDERFUL DAY

I was having a wonderful day,
I also met a guy named Ray.
He said hi,
But I said bye.
That is what happened to me today.

I woke up the next day,
I think it was sometime in May.
It was a nice sunny day,
I met Dr. Dray.
So he gave me a check-up,
Then I got back up.
So I started to drive away.

John Newman
Age: 9

THE REAL THINGS

Dogs bark,
Cats meow,
The dog that was barking was a chow.
The car horn was beeping,
But I was peeping,
And my brother was sleeping,
But my mother was weeping.

Sarah Sheehan
Age: 9

THERE'S A MONSTER IN MY ATTIC

There's a monster in my attic,
It's very very big.
Last night he crept downstairs,
And stole my stuffed animal pig.
He looks sort of scary,
And has a purple nose.
Once his shaggy fur got wet,
When I sprayed him with the hose.
Even though he stamps a lot,
I am not afraid of it.
Because last year for my birthday,
I received a capturing kit.
So last night I sneaked upstairs,
While everyone was asleep.
I caught that monster with my rope,
And holding I did keep.
He looked at me with a sad little face,
Suddenly I felt sorry for him.
So I untied my rope,
And now he's my best friend Tim.

Kathie Zipp

NATURE

The trees can be green,
Their colors are always seen,
Red, golden, and green.

Santino Galizio
Age: 10

THE SKY IS DARK

the sky is dark
the stars are bright
the moon is out
and I am to sleep good night

Brittany Dietz
Age: 7

MY DAD

My dad was once a funny man
But he never ate anything out of a can
He never would cry
But he always had to say good-bye
To his pretty wife named Jan

Bobby Meholif

ANSWERS HELD BACK

it seems we forget how to live
in the quickness of our haste
there's no need to point the finger
so we look for other ways
as virtue slipped into my shoe
our lives were rearranged
the pain grows fast and rigid
like the blood coursing through my veins
i looked for some answers
but there were none to be found
so i turned to my angel
who stranded me on the ground
while gossip burns on the tip of your tongue
and little whispers circle around your head
before you judge me, take a look at you
i see faith in your eyes
and strength in your hands
never you hear the discouraging lies
so please understand
the healing hand held back by the deepened nail
follow the God that i failed

David Kirk Hull
Age: 16

WRITER'S BLOCK

Once again I sit down to write
With paper and pen in my sight
My English teacher has just assigned
Another poem of at least eight lines
I am anxious and excited to do this well
Any minute the thoughts will swell
Two hours have passed the page is white
This assignment is ruining my night
My heart is pounding in my ears
I know I'm on the verge of tears
EUREKA I'VE GOT IT
I'm on the right track
Oh forget it I'm going for a snack

Angelle Zakaib
Age: 11

SPRINGTIME

It is always nice to see the dead trees
Come to life with little green leaves.
With the sunshine the leaves will grow
Into a beautiful glow.
From the window you see the rain
It won't be long before you are outside playing a game.

Violet Cashman
Age: 11

HALLOWEEN

Signs of Halloween are seen here and there.
Cute costumes and creepy creatures are everywhere.
When the clock strikes 6:00 it's time to go.
Dressed in costume we're ready to show!
Scary sounds through the night,
Screaming and screeches fill me with fright.
The warm apple cider and candy corn are great.
They make Halloween worth the wait!

Laura C. Hopkins

THE NIGHTMARE ON HALLOWEEN NIGHT!

On Halloween night,
It's such a fright!
Witches hide in ditches,
Frankenstein has stitches!
Ghosts pop out to boast,
To have a Halloween toast!
Skeletons dance with mummies,
They drink punch and eat gummies!
Children run around and scream,
Is this all a dream?

Rachael Annes
Age: 10

LEAVES ARE FALLING

You see leaves everywhere,
Crunching under your feet,
They might even get caught in your hair,
But they look so neat,
They are falling continuously on the ground,
Swirling all around,
They could be shaped like a star,
Or even a candy bar,
Their size could be little and small,
Or they could be big and tall,
This is the season we call fall.

Meredith Mead
Age: 10

GHOST TOWN

Ghost town is a place you don't want to be.
It's chilly and a bit scary to me.
As the old woman sits in her chair
she knits all day long, sometimes
singing or humming a song.
The sheriff of town uses his blood hound
tracking crooks who are trying not to make a sound.
If he is shot with a bullet of a gun he begins to bleed.
Then he rides away on his trusty brown steed.

Alec Faulhaber
Age: 10

BE TRUE TO YOURSELF

Always look on the bright side of things,
   and really see what life has to bring.
Don't sit in the dark at night and worry,
   otherwise your life will be over in a hurry.

Don't be afraid to be who you are,
   you are the only one of you, by far.
No one is perfect, we've all got a flaw,
   so go out and make all of those people awe.

You may not be pretty, athletic, or smart,
   but that doesn't mean that you cannot start.
Don't let peers cause you to fall,
   if you ever need a friend, just call.

Step out into the world and yell,
   I am me and that's just swell.
I love being me, for who I am,
   because we each, are a special gem.

I keep a smile on my face,
   and feel that I'm full of grace.
So live your life as full as can be,
   and always remember, you can call on me.

Christine Newman
Age: 13

ONE TRUE FRIEND

A friend is one who's on your side;
Who'll comfort you after you've cried.
One who calms you if you're mad
And turns depressing days to glad.

A friend is there through thick and thin
Caring, concerned, and genuine.
A special someone with the gift
To give your heavy heart a lift.

When you're down and in despair,
A faithful friend is always there.
They do not scold but lend a hand
And always seem to understand.

A friend always shops with you at the store
And always makes you smile more.
A friend is full of love and care.
This kind of friend is always rare.

So, if you have but one true friend
To be there for you to the end,
Thank the Lord and say a prayer;
'Cause you're richer than a millionaire!

Mai Ngo

ANGELS

Angels are guardians with wings
They wear white, carry harps, and sing
They watch over your shoulder
They make sure you're warm, and never get colder
They care for you, each and every day
They protect you, and they pray
Angels sing lovely songs
They fill your hearts with joy, so nothing will go wrong
They are messengers, sent by God
They stick together like three peas in a pod
They watch over you when you sleep
They make sure you never weep
They help you through everything
They make the chimes in Heaven ring

Courtney Musarra

THE FUN NIGHT

P retty costumes roam streets.
U ncle Gary takes me trick-or-treat.
M y baby cousin comes too.
P retty leaves are so fun.
K ids are happy to be outside.
I n my house there is a party.
N ew kids are at my party.

Sabrina Rakosy
Age: 8

WHAT IS A FRIEND...

A friend is a person who is always there,
A friend is a person who will always care.
She will always be true, honest, and fair,
And always compliment on your hair.

A friend is a person you can always count on
Through thick and thin
Through boys and all in every season straight
Through fall.

A friend will never go behind your back,
They will always cut you slack.
Friends will always share their feelings,
So I make sure I am always there.

Amanda Coyne
Age: 12

LIFE

Life is good,
Life is fine,
Your's is great and so is mine.
We go through life but only once,
So make the most of it,
And don't be a dunce.

Katie DiCostanzo
Age: 9

THANKSGIVING

Thanksgiving is a time for joy;
   for every girl and boy.

It's time for happiness and cheer;
   and for all families to be near.

It is time for fun:
   from which is never done.

It's time to eat turkey;
   just don't drink water if it's murky.

It's time for everyone to do their best;
   and when it's all over it's time to rest.

Paul Lyons
Age: 14

RAINBOW

Rainbow
multicolored
shows itself when it rains
gives you a gay feeling inside
Bright arch

Zephylia Khooblall
Age: 10

A CRUSH

One day you meet someone,
Someone who is a guy,
And though you can't describe it,
You feel weird when he walks by.

You look at him and smile,
And he smiles back at you,
And then you sit and wonder,
If he really likes you too.

You talk about him constantly,
On each and every day,
But sometimes you can't help it,
You have so much more to say.

You sit there during school,
And write his name on books,
You just can't pay attention,
Because of his good looks.

Sometimes you get depressed,
Your head just starts to swirl,
You don't think that he likes you,
It seems like the end of the world.

You don't know what to think,
Because everyone you know,
Tells you that he likes you,
But it really doesn't show.

You're feeling really nervous,
You can't just ask him out,

But if you don't you'll never know,
Just what this is about.

It's just a situation,
That could go either way,
He could either say he likes you,
Or he could just say no way.

Nicole Kubinski
Age: 13

SLEDDING

During the winter I love to sled,
But it makes you dog-tired and you feel dead.
Your boots feel like they're full of lead,
Your knees are wobbly and your face is red.

When I get inside I try to rest,
But I haven't got to the part I like best.
I make myself some hot hot tea,
And then I go to sleep you see.

That is what I do a lot,
It really hits me on the spot.
You may like it or you may not,
But this is what I do a lot.

Evan Sheha

MY FAVORITE FOOD!

It's such a treat
to have good things to eat.

I get a tickle
when I eat a pickle.

I start to pout
if I don't get my sauerkraut.

I use my favorite fork
to eat lots of pork.

My heart sings
when I see dumplings.

I sure am keen
when it comes to green beans.

Colby and cottage if you please
these are my favorite kinds of cheese.

Instead of red tomatoes
I'd rather mashed potatoes.

I act kind of jerky
until I get a lot of turkey.

There's absolutely nothing
like the taste of stuffing.

I don't give a hoot
about any kind of fruit.

I can always take
a nice piece of cake!

Leeanne R. Taylor
Age: 10

BASKETBALL

Basketball is fun
It's a very active sport
Dribble, shoot, and pass

Brigid Patton
Age: 11

TRICK-OR-TREAT

Halloween is almost here
It is the scariest time of the year.
Big orange jack-o'-lanterns are lit up bright.
Demons and goblins come to give you a fright!

Rachel Jimenez

POOH BEAR RAP

There's Eeyore, Piglet, Pooh and Roo,
Many many more loved by me and you!
Eeyore's always, always down in the shed,
When he gets back up he'll bump his head!
Piglet is a little scaredy pig,
He'll always always wish he was so big!
Tigger is a big bouncing grr,
He'll never never wait until his turn!
Little young Roo is a trouble shoe,
He'll act like a cow and go moo moo moo!
Gopher is a real "diggin'" machine,
He'll dig up your house right after you cleaned!
Rabbit is a real harvester,
He'll make some soup and go stir stir stir!
Owl is a real smart hoot,
He'll give you the measures of a straight down shoot!
Last but the best is our own Pooh,
He's way way better than some old shoe!
So that's the end of our Pooh Bear Rap,
So it's time to say bye and clap clap clap!

Marina Bach
Age: 10

A POEM CALLED NATURE

Nature is so silent
it shows you what
a lovely creation
the Lord God has made.

Nature is a thing
that is always around
you so take time
to just look at it.

Nature is a beauty to me
so take time to look around
and whatever you like
must be a part of "Nature".

Nature is not something
that you should just listen too,
you should open your two eyes
and look at it.

Gregory Perez

CHRISTMAS DAY

All I can see is the color white,
It sparkles and shines ever so bright,
Trees swaying and creaking as the wind blows,
No noise from the squirrels as they doze.

No birds singing in the trees,
No songs carrying with a breeze,
The trickling spring is a sheet of ice,
Thoughts of swimming are not so nice.

This is a quiet time of year,
Nothing for miles and miles to hear,
Yet I sense some excitement in the air,
As if everyone is preparing to go to a fair.

Can you guess what time of year it is?
It is a favorite for all the kids,
Someone comes wearing a big red suit,
He also has a fluffy white beard
And a pair of black boots.

We get to stay home from school,
I get to sleep in and watch TV, that's cool,
But most important, a day we can't forget,
Jesus' birthday for which
We will always be in God's debt.

Kristen Bergman
Age: 10

MY GUARDIAN ANGEL

There's a guardian angel by my side
I know that for sure she is my guide
Through right things and wrong
She will guide me to the right way
Margaret or Charlotte might be her name
I know she is with me for I can tell
Her hand is on me when I do well

Charlotte Bacho
Age: 12

TIGGER

Tigger the tiger is a friend of Pooh.
When Tigger jumps he is bigger than you.

Tigger the tiger is a really weird cat.
He does not like honey and you cannot change that.

Tigger the tiger is one of a kind
Sometimes I think he has lost his mind.

Tigger the tiger can be scary at times,
Especially to Piglet who he scares out of his mind.

He has friends, Rabbit, Kanga, Roo,
Eeyore, Piglet and Pooh.
But his best friend could be you.

Ami Ignatious
Age: 10

CHRISTMAS

Christmas is like cold
with snow on the ground.
The snow is the fun part.

Christmas is about Jesus
who is born on Christmas.

On Christmas morning
you get presents
from your mom and dad.

Christmas is the time
to enjoy your family
by going over to
Grandma's house.

Then you will see
how we all sit and talk
and have a lot of
celebration.

Ryan Helderman
Age: 10

There once was a man,
Who didn't like to do track
But he loved to swim.

James 'J.D.' Vasko
Age: 11

PRETENDING

Sometimes when I am lonely,
  feeling sad and blue,
I pretend that I am happy
  and sitting next to you.
Or when I fall and hurt my knee,
  and feel really sad,
I just pretend that you are with me
  and start to feel glad.
Or if I'm feeling kind of scared,
  when I'm at home alone,
I pretend that we're together
  and eating ice cream cones.
So if you're feeling sad, or scared,
  or even kind of mad,
Just pretend I'm there and then,
  maybe you won't feel so bad.

Audrey Kisilewicz
Age: 11

FLUBBER

Flubber is colorful, bouncy and wet
Maybe I can take it to the vet
And trade it in for another pet
Can I give it to you?
No, because I am new
Well, then let me put you in my stew
Its name is Abby
Be careful because she is saggy
Or maybe she is Danny
Read her a book
On a hook
And let her cook.

Tamara Celina Manrique
Age: 8

APPLE

Once there was an apple,
Who hung up in a tree.

It was very free,
Since it hung up in a tree.

One day a worm came and ate it up,
And the next day, the apple, you -- could not see.

Kelly Camp

MY CAT

My cat has a hat
The next day he was fat
I could not see him in a fog
Then I saw a dog

Richard J. Cegonko Jr.
Age: 8

SHE CAME OUT

She came out yellow,
She came out blue
She came out saying I love you.
She came out mean,
She also came out too lean.
She came out gold
Holding a big fat mold and rolled.
She came out red and thought she was dead
Until she met me and my brothers,
Ted, Fred, and Ed.
She came out brown to touch the ground
And soon she made us frown.
She came out black
And said, "I'll be right back."
When she came out pink we didn't blink
See ya, we'll be right back, I think.

Christina Louise Oravec
Age: 8

YEEK

Yeek! I've got a paper with rhyming words you see.
Oh no! What do I write? Trouble is here for me.
I'll think and think and think. I'll be here until I'm old.
Why is it so hard, poetry is easy so I've been told.
I'll sit at my desk pondering, 'til I'm forty-two.
I'll sit at my desk wondering
'Til the world ends and the skies aren't blue.
I'll probably die of explosion and I'll turn into goo!
I can only hope this madness won't happen to you!

Colleen Maher
Age: 9

BASEBALL

I like baseball
It's very cool
You don't have to be tall
To play baseball

It is very fun
You get to run
You could hit the ball
Over the wall
That is why I like baseball

John Palumbo
Age: 12

BASKETBALL

Basketball is fun,
Because you have to run,
It is great,
Because when you play they treat you first rate,
In the game,
You don't have to play
Like you're playing in the Hall of Fame,
True, when you play you need water,
But you need it to slaughter the other team,
So, that's why I like basketball,
Sometimes you hardly don't fall,
But to me, it is the best of all!

Sara Perez
Age: 11

MY SANDWICH

I opened my lunch box and what did I find?
A sandwich! My oh, my what a crime
It had salami, tuna, mustard too
Ketchup, lettuce and onions, phew!
I would trade anything for my sandwich, glue
Scissors, even a marker if I had to
When I went home to my mother
I complained to her that there was no butter

Lyndsey Gall
Age: 8

BATS

Bats are neat.
Bats are cool.
Some people might think they are ghouls.
They sleep during the day,
So they won't be the prey.
During the night,
They swoop this way and that,
To catch a fly, moth, or a gnat.
They live in caves, old houses, and such,
Where they leave much, much, mush.
Bats use an echo to catch flying bugs,
All the while baby bats hang on their mothers
With a big hug.

Mark German
Age: 11

MOP TOP

Someone had to mop
Then someone found a top
Then someone didn't have a mark
Someone went to the store to buy tops
Then someone went to the store to buy mops
Then someone went to the park

Nicholas Baur
Age: 8

HARMONY

All humans in existence should live in harmony.
Black or white, short or tall, it doesn't really matter.
If an enemy is climbing a ladder,
One shouldn't push him off.
No fighting, lying, stealing,
Any of that makes me scoff!
We're all in this world together.
We should make it a better place.
If we fight against each other,
If we fight another race,
We surely wouldn't have a chance,
To survive with togetherness.
We wouldn't be able to fill our lungs with oxygen,
Without feeling someone's stealing our air.
We'd be lost without each other.
We'd be greedy, selfish -- jealous of our own mother.
Is that the way you want to live?
Do you want to be a disgrace?
Our world would fall apart without peace and harmony,
So please, think before you tease someone,
Or fight and injure another.
When someone's hurt and you don't think to bother,
Just remember this poem
And think about living in harmony.

Keriann Hurst
Age: 10

THE GHOST

I have a ghost
and it calls me the host.
Its name is Renegade
and it likes lemonade.
He's a great cook
and he likes books.
He likes Kit-Kat bars
and drives imaginary cars!

Joel Meister
Age: 9

MARY'S DISGUSTING SECRET

Mary has a disgusting secret,
That you don't want to know about,
When she thinks nobody's looking,
She shoves her finger up her nose,
Because of this she has no friends,
Now she's doing back bends,
She's turning sad,
And becoming mad,
If she wants her friends back,
She's going to have to learn an issue,
That would be,
To use a tissue!

Ashley Tamas
Age: 10

THE TREE

I gaze out my window at the tree
It's incongruous with the others
Other trees are wispy and feathery
I could reach out and snap them in half
This tree is stronger, it stands out
The tree has a dense trunk holding it up with pride
The long gnarled branches show years of harsh wind
Bitter winds whipping and whirling around the branches
One of the branches sends a chill down my spine
It's like an old witch beckoning me to her
Or a wild cat's claw striking his adversary
I see the tree in many perspectives
It can be like a mother, stable and warmhearted
In another light
It's a valiant knight protecting his people
This tree has a queer grip on me
Every time I turn away I can feel it
I can feel it calling me back
Of course I have no choice, but to twirl around
I stare at this tree every day now
Every day I notice something new
Something new every day

Jessie Bigelow
Age: 11

DAVID JUSTICE

David Justice hits home runs
touches home plate.
Because of him and Matt Williams
we won the pennant.
We also got to the World Series
and that's the way we play.

Michael Koh
Age: 9

SNOW FLURRIES

Snow is falling from the sky,
It is falling, oh, my!
I think summer is dying right before my eyes.
I will miss the warm summer cries,
Of the sparrows when I snuggle in bed!
Good-bye summer, I don't care about you.
I WANT snow, oh, yes I DO!!

Snow is falling from the sky,
It is falling, oh, my!
Everything is dying,
Everyone is crying,
Because winter has come!
Good-bye summer I don't care about you.
I WANT snow, oh, yes I DO!!

Lindsay Peck
Age: 10

WINTER

Oh how I love winter
Because it's my birthday
It's so so cold I jiggle a wiggle
I slip and slide
I don't know why
I just love winter.

Samantha Fitzpatrick
Age: 8

THIS LITTLE GIRL

This is the girl that walks the streets of Putting Bay.
That walks the dog Scruffie that got away.
Who lost her bow along the way.
When looking found an apple astray.
Then came a loud crump!
And it went down with a gump!
This girl was very polite.
So, she tightened her lips very tight.
This little girl tripped on a stone.
She got up and groaned.
This little girl saw something red as the sea.
Red as her head.
It turned out to be, this little girl found her bow.
That was deep in the snow.

Stephanie Tucker
Age: 9

THE KISS

The kiss of the sun
gives us warmth.

The kiss of the moon
lays us to sleep.

The kiss of the sky
gives us freedom.

The kiss of the clouds
brings us dreams.

The kiss of the flowers
gives us beauty.

The kiss of the wind through the trees
gives us a whisper.

The kiss of the owl
brings us wisdom.

The kiss of the birds
gives us melody.

The kiss of the universe
gives us life.

Nick Spinelli
Age: 11

GOD IS ALWAYS WITH US

God is always with us,
  Whenever we get lost.
And when we fail,
  He helps us no matter what the cost.

God is always with us,
  All day and all night.
And when we are in trouble,
  He helps us see the light.

God is always with us,
  Whenever we need support.
It doesn't matter
  If we're black or white, tall or short.

God is always with us,
  No matter what our need.
Sometimes all it takes,
  Is for Him to plant the seed.

God is always with us,
  When we give a helping hand.
And by doing this,
  We are following His command.

Stephanie Yanok
Age: 10

HALF DOG/HALF MONKEY

We got two new puppies today.
Our Old Lady Pup Chelsea,
after fourteen years, she passed away.
It was a sad day.

These two puppies are really spunky,
I think they are half dog/half monkey.

These puppies are sisters.
One is Misty,
the other is Sable.
They're always running
under the kitchen table.

Puppies run, jump, climb and play,
Misty ate my school speller yesterday.

Sable ate my history book today,
Mr. "J", my teacher said
"Jason, that's O.K.,
in the spring,
your parents will pay."

My dogs are really bad,
so don't make them mad.

For if you do, you will see...
why they are half dog/half monkey.

And at the end of the day,
when they're not so spunky
they can be warm and cuddly

and oh so funny,
my half dog/half monkeys.

I love them.

Jason Werden
Age: 12

FLOWERS AND BEES

I picked a flower I put it in a vase
The vase broke so I put it on a base
Underneath the vase the base broke
I didn't know what to do so I put
The flower back and cried, "Boohoo."
Then I saw a bee, "Ouch, it stung me."
The bee died and another bee came
And landed on the flower then landed on me
But it didn't sting me.
The bee flew away and I ran inside
I took a walk and waved, "Bye, Bye."
When I came back I found a surprise.
It was a party! But nobody was there.
Then everyone jumped out to shout surprise!
"Happy birthday" everyone said.
I got a present. It was a dog.
So, now, I pet his paws.

Kathryn Robinson
Age: 8

THE CAT

My cat will not stop meeeowing.
No, no cat, don't meeeow.
Meeoowww said my cat.
STOP NOW!
I wish he would stop meeeowing.

Michael Hromco
Age: 7

AUTUMN

In autumn you do
lots of things
Like raking the
Orange, yellow, brown, and red leaves.

Then put them in a bonfire.
So you can have a wiener roast
and roast marshmallows.

Some times there
are festivals, hayrides,
camp-outs, and football games.
And I always love
to jump in the leaves.

Megan H. Lee
Age: 10

HALLOWEEN

I like Halloween because it is fun,
And I like to get candy and gum.
I know this is not funny,
But it is yummy.
When I went home there was none.

Shane Susanek
Age: 8

Cats,
Cats,
Cats,
Cute cats
Marvelous, pretty cats
Happy, sad, sleepy cats
Big cats
Small cats and kitty cats
Fat, skinny cats
Bad, nice, silly cats
Striped cats, too
Girl cats, women cats
Boy cats, men cats
Don't forget baby cats
Last of all --
Best of all,
I like copycats

Elizabeth Buck
Age: 8

THE OWL

Mating season, the owls fly,
really high in the black night sky.
Eating critters such as mice,
are very, very nice.
Coughing up bones, feathers, and fur,
making up a neat ball.
It is sad to know critters die,
and it might cause some pain,
but just remember it's part of a chain,
a food chain.

Kevin Seiler
Age: 11

THE STORMY DAY

Rain falls from the sky,
Just like tears from my eye,

Clouds are placed way up high,
Like cotton growing in the sky,

The sky is dark and very gray,
It is such a dark and dreary day,

What do these have in common you say,
This is what you see on a stormy day.

Jamie Craft
Age: 12

IF

Wouldn't it be great, wouldn't it be cool,
if you could be a little different,
and not be called a fool.
Everyone had a house and everyone ate:
Smiles were always real, and never fake.
Wouldn't it be cool, wouldn't it be fun,
if you didn't burn your feet while you
were walking on the sun.
Wouldn't it be great if the world was different.
Wouldn't it be great if our lives were too.
Wouldn't it be great if you gave love,
and love always came back to you.
Wouldn't it be great if that were true.
If.

Jodi Schwaben
Age: 12

CHIEF

I have a huge gorilla named Chief,
His favorite food is a side of beef,
In the jungle we met,
Now he's my pet,
And his job is to scare away every thief.

Evan Yoak
Age: 12

GETTING DIRTY

Getting dirty is a mess
Getting dirty means use Zest

Getting dirty is like mud
They both are a lot of fun

Getting dirty makes Mom mad
Getting dirty is like a fad

Getting dirty is so fun
It's a laugh that always runs

Jeremy A. Oberdove
Age: 12

CHASE

Along this twisted path I go
Along this turning trail of woe
Not stopping once to pause and peek
As I splash across a creek
Cannot stop and take a look
Must flee to my cozy nook
Too cautious to turn around
To meet sharp teeth of hunting hound
Never stop always run
From the hunter, hound, and gun.

Katelyn Radack
Age: 11

JACK FROST

Chilly, cold outside
Warmth inside a little house
Fire on the stove

Michael Nihiser
Age: 12

CAT

There once was a very cool cat.
He lost change whenever he sat.
He became very poor,
Bought no toys at the store,
so, he sat down and cried like a brat!

Matt Lukwinski
Age: 12

CAT

Once there was a little cat
It sat on a big baseball bat
It was so big
It looked like a fig
And its name was Matt

Esther Leung

GENTLE BREEZE

A gentle breeze drifts,
It glides like skaters on ice,
And flows gracefully.

Ashley Gercevic

Dog
eating, sleeping, weeping
german shepherd, hound, siamese, lion
eating, loving, sleeping
black, small
Cat

Larry Ritchie
Age: 11

Trick-or-treat on Halloween night,
  Kids in costumes on the streets.
Pumpkins shining by candle's light,
  Babies and teenagers begging for sweets.
It was supposed to be a night of horror,
  But to me, at least, it was just a bore.

Aaron Longstreth

TEARS

Tears are like waterfalls
of sadness that fall
from people of loss.

Tears are like dewdrops,
the little droplets
on the little faces.

Tears are like rain.
Rain makes a
gloomy day gloomy.

When the tears are over
They are like a rainbow that
has formed on the person's face.

Elizabeth A. Bruno
Age: 12

SUPERMAN

It's a bird it's a plane no it's a man,
He better watch out or he'll hit that van,
Look he's flying like a butterfly,
That sure is a pretty, strange guy,
No wait look closer it, it's SUPERMAN!!

Joe Whitacre
Age: 11

HOMEWORK

Homework, homework,
I hate homework.
Homework is a pain.
I wish that I could skip it,
and
go to the Pizza Hut.
I wish
but it probably won't come true.

Rachel Harris
Age: 7

One day
I saw
a leaf
falling off
slowly off
a tree
that is
so plain
that it
felt like
time has
stopped right
in its
continuous tracks

Don Xu
Age: 12

ME AND MY COUSIN

Me and my cousin live far apart,
We don't live close at all.
Sometimes we get lonely,
So I give her a call.

We talk about
how we are doing,
what we do in school,
and we plan a day we could get together
I think that would be cool.

We can write to each other
because our moms and dads
work in the same place.
We love each other a lot and I miss her.

Tara Honsaker
Age: 6

ME AND YOU

Me and you.
We love to play up in the mountains
Up up and away we run
Skip, jump, and fall
We play until our families call.

Alexa M. Bull
Age: 6

SCHOOL IS FUN!

School is cool.
School is the best,
best place yet.
But when we are off
it is no fun at all.
And when I have the
best teacher yet
school can be
fun, fun, fun!
But when the year goes
you leave your teacher,
But you can still talk to her.
School, school, school.
I like school.
I like school and you
make lots of friends
and I think you can only make
friends in school.
School again.
School, school, school.
School rules,
Yay school!

Stacey Hromco
Age: 8

THE CAT WENT TO GRANDMA'S

The cat went to Grandma's.
It met a dog.
They were best friends.
Their names were Anna and Stacey.
They will always be best friends!

Anna Christine Bose
Age: 7

SCHOOL

School is cool.
Why does our principal rule the school?
School is fun.
Do you like school?
School, school, school.
I love school!
School is the best.
I think my school is the best.
I like the principal very very much.
At school you can make friends.
That will be fun!

Rachel Weitzel
Age: 7

SEALS

Seals, seals, I love seals!
I see them jumping,
jumping up in the air.
I see them play ball on their noses.
They are very funny.
Sometimes you see them in circuses!
They live in the water with other seals,
like their father and their mother.
They catch fish for their prey.
They eat them.
MMmmmm mmmmm.
They are tasty!
Seals, seals, I just love seals!

Amanda Carlyon
Age: 7

MOM MET THE CAT AND THE BAT

The mom loved the cat.
And along came a bat.
The mom didn't know what to do with the bat.
So she named it Matt.
And that was that.

Emma Schilling
Age: 6

C ool
O h, I am awesome
L ittle and cute
L ollipops
I mportant
N eat!

Collin Arnold
Age: 7

GROUNDED

I knew I shouldn't have stole the cookie,
or on testing day played hookie.
Because of course my mom caught me,
and grounded me you see.
So I guess when it comes to pranks, I'm still a rookie.

Daniel Brown

THE GOATS

On Monday
goats came into my backyard
and digged up my flowers.
I brought them into my house
and they messed up the house.
So we put them to bed.
Good night, goats!

Rachel Goodrich
Age: 6

SCHOOL

School, school,
I love school.
School is cool.
School rules!
Do you like school?
School is fun.

What is your favorite thing about school?
My favorite thing about school is my teacher.
Do you like your teacher?
School is the best!

Eryn Edgerton
Age: 7

COOL SCHOOL

There was a cool school,
   That was pretty cool.
It did not have any rules,
   But it was full of fools.
It was still a cool school.

Cameron Willson
Age: 9

A BOY

Once there was a boy,
Who liked the color brown.
He was very thin and tall,
And liked to play basketball,
So he went to see a game in town.

Daniel Kaib

WINTER

Winter is a special time,
From Christmas to giving a Valentine.
The birds have all gone south,
And you won't catch flies in your mouth.
Gone are the days for sunbathing,
Now it's time for ice-skating.
Snow and sleet add to our fun,
But, oh sun when will you come!

Jay Thomas
Age: 10

POEMS

Which one to use,
there's so many to choose.
Poems bring laughter,
sometimes tears right after.
Poems can be possessive,
and some may be depressive.
Some may be useful,
thoughtful or truthful.
Some are imaginative,
others just touch the soul.
Or a poem can be
Just a poem............so I'm told

Brittany Rae Behanna
Age: 11

THE COOL KID

There was a cool kid,
His name was Sid.
He worked on a farm,
And lived in a barn.
He bought a horse and named it Vid.

Brianne Dishong
Age: 8

THE POOL

There was a pool,
That was cool.
Once a kid jumped in,
To take a swim.
And got caught by a ghoul.

Tyler R. Ellis

PENCILS

I write with pencils.
I always write with them.
I don't know why?
It is fun writing with markers and pens and crayons.
But most of all I write with pencils.
I don't care if everyone else likes to color with markers
or pens or crayons.
I just like pencils most of all.
I think it is fun using pencils.

Ashley M. Kruczek
Age: 8

WRITER'S BLOCK

Thinking of something to write.
Lost in my own world.
Actually, I lost myself
After I was finished writing my name.

What shall I write about?
Should I write about dogs, cats, lions, tigers,
Or bears?
Oh my!!
I wonder when I shall find myself again.

Tara Mitchell
Age: 11

POTHOLES OF LIFE

Along life's weary, winding highway,
One hits a shallow mundane pit,
That pockmarks every road and byway,
Waiting to send a pedestrian to reel and flip.
How bothersome, they, to the laissez-faire
Forced to work and take detours,
But ever more loathsome to those who care
For experience and its tantalizing lures.
Potholes delay and make short work
Of our careful, well-laid plans.
Torture it is to watch them smirk,
Dictating our small can't and cans.
I wish to cease dealing with their malevolence
To be only concerned with matters of significance.

Alex Stefaniak
Age: 14

IN FALL

In the FALL,
I have a ball.
To hop on top of leaves.
And fall like a wall.
Are you going on a trip?
We'll see you next FALL!

Douglas Watt
Age: 9

SOLITARY TREE

On a hill, a tree stands all alone,
With the moon behind its branches.
The monolithic presence is superior
To all surrounding it.
Reaching upward,
Naked branches seem to touch the sky,
With pitch-black bark as dark as night.
The tree stands alone,
With no living thing anywhere.
No man has ever touched or tended it.
Nor was it harmed by the red flower
That turned things to ash.
The tree stands abandoned,
Defying everything.
Nothing dares to ever go near.
The blackened bark has no virtue left,
No memory of spring rains
Gently caressing its leaves and skin.
No memory of the sun shining on it,
As it stood in a river of green.
The tree stands alone,
A dead tree on a blackened hill.

Andrew Stefaniak
Age: 10

JACK-O'-LANTERN

A jack-o'-lantern,
has a very scary face
it glows bright at night.

It is very nice,
to have a jack-o'-lantern
on Halloween night.

Faces of all kinds,
merry, scary, or hairy
lit with candlelight.

Smooth on the outside,
gooey, ooey filled with seeds
that's the way it is.

Trick-or-treat is fun,
but when the bright light goes out
the night fun is done.

Allison Parker
Age: 9

An August moon
A perfect sky
Blue like six miles underwater
Melting west to a deep mauve.
Silhouettes of trees standing out
Against the constant sparkle
Of lightning bugs.
The soft, cool, gentle air
Hangs sweetly and perfectly
Around me.
The quiet foreshadowing of fall
Seems almost tangible, yet out of reach.
Fall is in no hurry.
It takes its time as
August lingers.

Amanda Hartman
Age: 15

FALL

In fall it's a little chilly.
All the beautiful colors like green and red.
It is a good time for friends to come over.
You could jump in the leaves.
That is much fun.
I like fall a lot.
I think you will like it too!

Matthew Milla
Age: 8

INDIANS

Jaret Wright: Does his best as a righty.
Jose Mesa: Has the pitch.
Jim Tome: Takes the point.
Omar Vizquel: Has the move.
Paul Assenmacher: Has the stance.
Sandy Alomar, Jr.: Has the signs.
Orel Hershiser: Is a dog.
Charles Nagy: Has the look.
Manny Ramirez: Has the hit.
David Justice: Has the arm.

Branden Stucky
Age: 8

PUMPKINS

I like pumpkins,
Big or little, fat or thin.
I like pumpkins any size!
I like their little faces.
Some are cute, some are sad.
Some are scary, some are mad,
And happy, too.
I like pumpkins' stems too because
They can be curly or straight.
I pick my pumpkin by all of these things,
And then I think up a face for it.

Krysta Pesarchick
Age: 8

Goblins! Goblins! Everywhere!
Don't get them in your hair.
You might get a fright,
On Halloween night!

Matthew Tekaucic
Age: 8

SOFTBALL

The ball is big white and hard,
you'll need lots of yard.

Coach will give you a sign,
you'll try to do it just fine.

People will try to slide,
so be sure to tag them on the side.

If there's a fly ball,
don't let it fall.

Catch it for an out,
and the people will shout.

Slide at home and you might get sore,
but it's worth it as long as you score.

Tiffany A. Farr

FALL

Falling, falling to the ground
Falling, falling all around
Red, yellow, green and brown
Big and small crispy to the ground
Raking, raking on the ground
Raking, raking all around
Raking up the piles
From the trees that grow up miles
Some think it's a bore
Having to do that chore
But after you're done
You'll realize you had fun
Then you won't have to worry about mowing
'Cause it will be too busy snowing
After the snow leaves the ground
The trees begin to grow all around!

Jenny Reichart
Age: 12

Baseball
catch the ball, throw the ball
hit the ball, bunt the ball
hold the ball, play the ball
It's time to play ball
That's baseball

John Hausman

THE PIG THAT LEARNED TO FLY

I thought I'd never see
the day when pigs had
learned to fly,
but just last night what
did I see floating in
the sky?
A pig fat hog zooming
through the air,
Only stopping to do some
munching on descending Tupperware.
The pig kept me up all night
it was all that I could hear.
I was beginning to grow
deaf in my right ear.
It was then when I lost
what sanity I had.
I got up and screamed
"Shut up I want to go to bed!"
Well, my folks who were
up chattering in the very
next room thought it was them
that the scream was for.
So, ten seconds later, they
burst through the door,
screaming and hollering, with spit
flying on the floor.
Two days later when
my hearing was back, I told
them of the pig and the sky.

And as I grow old I still wonder why,
someone was dumb enough to
teach a pig to fly.

John Menefee
Age: 13

DADDY'S LITTLE GIRL

Once upon a time, he'd have given me the world,
Nothing was more important than Daddy's little girl.
We were so close and he was my best friend,
I thought it'd last forever,
Our good times would never end.
I cried when he packed his bags and went away,
He took a part of me with him when he left that day.
I'll never get that part back, it's gone forever,
The pain in my heart keeps making me remember.
All the many good times we shared,
I felt so happy to know he cared.
But when he left me, he broke my heart,
I can't understand why he's keeping us apart.
I often wonder if he's stopped loving me,
I'm curious to know if he's happy.
I need him in my life, need him to be there,
I need to know right now, does my dad still care?
When you're Daddy's little girl,
And comes that fateful day,
I wonder what you'd do when your daddy goes away.

Tiffany Ann Holes
Age: 16

There was a bush named Red
He had no leaves on his head,
He stood by a tree
Who laughed with glee,
So, he never go to go to bed.

Alison McGrady

MY FRIEND, MY CAT

Lost,
My dear friend
One in whom I trusted completely.
One who could not always ease my pain,
but suffered with me.
One who could not speak,
but always listened.
Gone,
My furry bundle of comfort.
Dear friend,
I told you that I loved you Kato,
but I wonder if I told you exactly
how much of my life you ruled.
And how much of my heart is still yours?

Elissa Marie Rump
Age: 11

CRAZY MAN

Crazy man in my home,
Here I am all alone.
Basement door left unlocked.
Oh my gosh, was I shocked.

Shifting here, shifting there,
Nevertheless, aware
That his movement I can see,
Is it him or is it me?

In the shadows lurks a danger,
A crazy, abnormal, psycho stranger.
A hook, a knife, or something strange,
Must belong to one deranged.

In fret and fear, anguish too,
I ran around, what should I do?
Will he kill me or will he not,
Would it take a single shot?

A monster appears upon the stairs,
Four legs, I can only stare.
I wobble on flimsy feet,
Before me I see.....Fluffy??

Dylan Kelly
Age: 11

FRIENDS

You always should have a good friend or two,
You even could have a friend that is new.
So when a new person arrives at your school,
Always run over and tell them they're cool.

An honest friend is a fine thing to be,
Or we could be great friends, as you can see.
Always remember be nice, don't be mean.
You still could be good friends when you are eighteen.

Tiffany Zepp
Age: 9

SNOWFLAKE

Snowflake,
Snowflake,
In the sky,
How I wish that I could fly.
You are so graceful
When you fall.
I am so clumsy,
I am so dull.
Snowflake,
Snowflake,
Could you please teach me?

Heather Piper
Age: 8

COME SEE MY GAME

My game is long and I might not play
For I am the person who sits down all day
I say I want to play
But they turn me down and put me away

Kelsey M. Allen
Age: 9

I see a monkey,
High in the trees,
Moving swiftly,
As fast as a bee.

On his face,
There is definitely not a frown,
He is showing a silly expression,
Like a clown's.

He is very slim,
Definitely not fat,
He is doing tricks now,
Like an acrobat.

He is very happy,
I can see,
He is just as happy,
As any monkey can be.

Danielle Sonntag
Age: 11

I JUST LOST MY APPETITE

Some people like beetles and bugs.
Some people just like to squish 'em.
Some people like to dish 'em,
And some people just think they're lugs.

I like bugs.
I hate to squish 'em.
And I hate to dish 'em
And bugs are definitely not lugs?

Do you like bugs?
Or do you squish 'em?
Or do you just like to plain dish 'em?
Or do you unfortunately think they're lugs?

Josiah R. Sprague
Age: 9

CATS

Cats
furry, pretty
jumping, playing, meowing
caring, soft, smooth, happy
Cat

Chelsea M. Edgecomb
Age: 9

CHILDREN ABOVE THE GROUND

Children above the ground
play here and there.
Do children above the ground
know how to be fair?

Children above the ground
do know how to be fair.
Children above the ground
care about insects down there.

Do the children above the ground
care enough to step aside
So the insects
don't have to hide?

Alex M. Tedrick
Age: 10

JENNY

There once was a girl named Jenny.
Who owned a lot of pennies.
She looked for the best buys.
She liked a lot of guys.
That silly girl Jenny.

Jenny Knauss

A MYSTERY OF NATURE

As autumn goes by...
Do the birds start to fly,
Do they go away to find,
The gleaming sunshine?

Yes, birds go away
As the leaves start to fall.
They fly south
In search of food for their babies mouths.

How do they know,
Which way to go,
Is it the breeze in the trees,
Or the power of the flower?

Meghan McGuire
Age: 9

BROWN

Brown leaves grow in town.
Brown leaves go on the ground.
They fall in fall.
That's why they call it fall.
In fall you can play ball
or call a friend
on the telephone in fall.

Amy Burke
Age: 8

ABOVE THE GROUND

Why do people drive in cars,
And drive all around the town,
Stop and get lots of gas,
And drive until their cars wear down?

People drive in cars so they're not late for things
And to get there fast,
Because we don't have wings,
And we hate getting there last.

What would we do without our vans,
Trucks, motor bikes and cars,
And how can we get around?
THANK GOD WE DON'T LIVE ON MARS!

Lea Dague
Age: 10

FALL

FALL is cold.
FALL is hot.
FALL is awesome to play in the leaves
Every day of the week.
Because I love FALL,
I can't wait until FALL comes around every year.

Brittney Lee Ratajczyk
Age: 8

HALLOWEEN

Halloween, Halloween
You do not eat a bean.

Ghost and goblins
And witches too
Lots of candy
For me and you!

Carved pumpkins
And scary thoughts,
Monsters running
All over the lots.

Full moons
And scary tunes,
Dressing up as
Silly baboons.

Hurry up, it's
Getting late,
Open the gate
To the last house
For the bait!

Brainne Holland
Age: 10

IMAGINATION

Wouldn't it be great if...
The clouds were made,
Of cotton candy, and sugar.
Then I could reach up,
Relax, and eat away.
I'd let my mind stray,
Into a magical place.
There are dragons and,
Dinosaurs, and lots of things,
That probably aren't real.
That magical place is my:

IMAGINATION!!!!!!

Stephnie Ann Bohon
Age: 10

PENCILS

Pencils.
They are fun.
You write, you draw with pencils.
Think if we didn't have pencils.
We couldn't draw, we couldn't write.
Pencils, pencils, they are fun.
Pencils, pencils, my poem is done.

Josh Wolny
Age: 8

WOULDN'T IT BE GREAT IF...

Gym was an hour
Things weren't sour
No one would die
And we could ALL fly.
Lunch was long
We could all play Ping-Pong
Baseball was all year
No one would drink beer
School was done
And we could all have some fun.

Mark Reifsnyder
Age: 11

OCTOBER

Even though October is cold,
I think October is fun
Because you can (if you want)
Jump in a pile of leaves
And when it starts getting colder,
You start carving pumpkins
And when you are done
You have a jack-o'-lantern and after that
You go trick-or-treating and when you're done
You go home and have supper
And have some treats from your bag.

Allyson Chlysta
Age: 8

THE SUN

Oh how I do love sunshine,
I've always wished it could be mine

The sun gives off such splendorous light,
I dread the time it becomes night

Through the clouds to my face,
I wish the sun wasn't in space

I wish it would come down to me,
Then I would take the key

I would open it up and jumped inside,
So that is where I would hide

I would hide from my sister, hide from my mom,
I would hide from my dad's favorite bomb

So that's how much I like the sun,
So now my poem is done

Brandi Colleen Bowser
Age: 11

SNOW

A big blanket covers me,
like a giant white sea.
I see a man, a white man.
He has a big top hat
and an orange nose,
a black mouth
how about that?
It is a snowman of course.

Brian Henry
Age: 9

HALLOWEEN

Halloween is the 31st
You eat candy until you burst
You dress up so you look scary
But walking down the streets can get hairy
You have to dress to trick-or-treat
But in late October, there's not much heat
Enjoy the pumpkins and all the hay
And always remember what to say
Trick-or-treat are the words you will hear
On the 31st of October each and every year

Kimberly Ann Starcher
Age: 9

BASEBALL

Shivers are tingling down my spine,
It's the bottom of inning nine.
There are two outs,
Three base runners no doubt,
When Coach put me up to bat.
Oh, what do you think of that?

Strike one! Strike two!
Oh, what do I do?!
Here come balls one, two, and three!
What's this? I've hit! Oh yes! Hee, hee!!
That GRAND SLAM came from me!

Chelsea Law
Age: 10

CHLOE

Chloe is my nutty dog.
she runs around all day.
She waits until I'm home from school
but then she wants to play.
She bites my toes,
but not real hard.
She gets into my stuff,
She never stops, until late at night
when she's finally had enough!

Jessica Joliat
Age: 9

THE SNOWY DAY

One Sunday it snowed
The snow was white and sparkly
We didn't have school
Our family went sledding
We don't have school tomorrow

Scott Barbone
Age: 9

MY PUMPKIN

My pumpkin.
My pumpkin.
So flat and round.
How I admire your roundness so round.
That's because you're my pumpkin.

Colton Piper

A TURTLE'S POINT OF VIEW

I crawl, I creep.
I squawk, I squeak.
I flee, I flow.
I row, I go.
I swim, I slide.
I grow, I glide.
I see danger, diddly dunk.
In my shell I go kerplunk!

Jesse D. Trillet
Age: 11

THE LAST

I broke free. Freedom. Crawling. Darkness.
I dig through the sand. Pebbly grains
Of sand. Light. Pouring light.
Streaming from above. I
Scrambled out of the
Sand, onto the sand.
The moist sand on my
Stomach. I'm out of breath.
In a flurry of flippers, I'm making
Progress. Wet. Waves. I'm prisoner of a crashing wave
Sea. Endless sea. Wet Water.
I wonder if any else have survived.
I wonder if I'm the last.
The last of the sea turtles.

Rebecca Orchard
Age: 10

91

CLEVELAND INDIANS

The Indians play at Jacobs Field.
When they come to bat the crowd never yields.

We had Kenny Lofton he is gone now,
But our left fielder: Justice make people say, "WOW!"

We acquired Matt Williams in a good trade.
And in batting he has it made.

We have Marquis Grissom, he steals lots of bases,
And he has played in many neat places.

We had a good season in '95,
We won one hundred games and our bats came alive.

Our "closer": Mesa had lots of saves,
We made the World Series but lost to the Braves.

We had a slugger, his name was Belle,
He is gone too, but still we do well!

Nagy's a pitcher who throws lots of strikes.
He's a pitcher that most people like.

We also have Ogea, he's pretty good too,
And the batters that face him get in a stew.

Alomar and Ramirez hit lots of home runs,
So the fans on the porch have lots of fun!

I love the Indians and all that they do,
And after reading this poem,
I hope you do too!

Go Tribe!

Jim Cochran
Age: 11

JANET

There was a planet,
By the name of Janet.
That had a ring,
That could sing.
That's all I can say about Janet the planet.

Michael Gercevic
Age: 8

WOODLAND SCHOOL

There was a dog at Woodland School,
The dog would always drool.
They would kick the dog out,
After they pet his snout.
Then the dog came back and said, "I am cool."

J. Hayden Harms
Age: 8

A
tear,
single and
solitary. Alone,
small, shed by the
clouds above. Do we
truly know? About our
history, our future, the vast-
ness of that around us? A lonely
tear, swallowed up by the ignorant
being as it swathed through what
was a mystery to its senses. Do
we truly know? Tears are
shed. Don't ignore them.
Or the tear's fate
Is yours.

Arland Rininger
Age: 13

FLUBBER/BLUBBER

There once was something green called flubber.
It bounded much like rubber.
It jumped and sprung,
It had much fun.
The flubber was much like rubber,
But it was somebody's blubber!

Alisan Russ
Age: 10

PEANUT

Small and brown
With a touch of gray
Still like a puppy
Loves to play.

Short little legs
A body that's long
Toenails that "click-clack"
As she waddles along.

We'll all love her dearly
To her final years
Which I am sure
Will cause many tears.

But until when
The Lord does call
We'll appreciate the love
She's given to all.

Megan Kreider
Age: 13

AN INNOCENT KILLER

A deafening scream escapes his throat
As he tears his razor sharp claws
Into the fur covered flesh of his victim.
A thick, red liquid pours out
Staining the snow-covered whiteness.
With a few flaps,
The victim is lifted from its bloody end
To a higher resting.
With a bone crushing grip,
What is left of the limp, lifeless body
Is ripped into pieces.
It goes to five rumbling stomachs
Perched high above the ground.

Amy Dexter

HAPPINESS

Happiness is like the snow falling on a cold winter day.
I see white snow and decorations all over the town.
I hear Christmas bells ringing and children singing.
I smell the smoke from fires coming out chimneys.
I touch the cold icy snow with my freezing hand.
I taste the cold winter snowflakes
Sprinkling into my mouth.

Jenna Baughman
Age: 10

HOPE IN DARKNESS

As like wandering in the dark,
nothing can be found.
As though these souls
And minds are like wandering in the dark,
Through out the universe,
Without anyone, or anything to comfort them.
Questions to be asked,
Without anyone to answer them.
It's like people just floating through life,
Without a purpose or a reason,
That they do not know --
Only the future can tell them,
But if they think that they're alone, they're wrong.
There's always someone with them at all times.

Abbie Gortner
Age: 13

HAPPINESS

Happiness seems pale pink.
Like a day on the Mediterranean.
I see the golden sun fill my house.
I hear the waves crash gently on the rocks.
I smell the scents of a warm summer day.
I touch the sparkling ocean water.
I taste the pure healthy air around me.

Megan Marie Wintersteller
Age: 11

HAPPY HALLOWEEN!!!

Go in the house if you dare,
I warn you, you're in for a scare.
My family is in there,
They want to watch you jump with fear.

Go in the house go in for fear,
My families in there waiting to scare.
I'll show you around if you dare,
But don't go to far in,
There they wait in all the dark corners.
They want to know if you want to join us.

Melissa Jones
Age: 11

HAPPINESS

Happiness is like neon yellow,
Like a bright summer day.
I see no gloomy clouds.
I hear happy birds singing.
I smell a lovely flower.
I touch little pricklies on my feet.
I taste the cool, sour lemonade.

Chrissy Dragovich
Age: 10

Halloween is here
We trick-or-treat everywhere.
Now the time has come to have fun.
We can dress up as goblins
And other spooky things.
But when the time comes again.
We can spook everyone again .
I will be waiting for a trick-or-treater .
When they come in I will have to eat them.
But when next year comes
I will have to spook again.

Tela Poling
Age: 12

ALONE

When I am home alone I think of you.
When I am in bed lying on my back
I look at the ceiling and think of my heart.

Gregory T. McDivitt

MY MOTHER

My mother lives in a big house
My mother has a big mouth
My mother has three kids
Their so sloppy they have to wear bibs.

My mother she laughs a lot,
And my mother thinks her kids are funny little tots.

My mother is nice
My mother likes to eat rice
My mother likes to joke
And that's all she wrote.

Cortney L. Summers

BUTTERFLIES

I saw them flying in the sky.
Tons of colors in the sky.
A beautiful butterfly.
Her named is Belle.
She had a boy named Bull.
I saw them one day.
Now they're gone forever.

Ashley Bartholdi
Age: 11

FRIENDS FOREVER

I will be your friend forever,
We are two peas in a pod,
We are inseparable,
When I am scared,
You make me brave,
When I am angry,
You make me laugh,
Laugh hard enough to make tears
Pour out of my eyes,
You will be my friend forever.

Some people ask, "Will you two ever separate?",
We say, "NEVER!",
We have our quarrels
But we always make up,
When you are sad,
I make you glad,
When you are in trouble
Or in a fight,
Girl I will be by your side,
We will be friends forever!!!!

Fiona Williams
Age: 12

'ROUND THE WORLD
LOOKING FOR MY CUDDLY FRIENDS

'Round the world and back again,
Looking for a cuddly friend.

Not a horse or not a mare,
I'm just looking for my teddy bear.
He is not under my bed,
Not on the shelf, oh, look
He is in the chair.

'Round the world and back again,
Looking for a cuddly friend.

Not a rat or a bat,
I'm looking for my little cat.
She is not on the floor,
Not climbing the curtains,
Oh, there she goes
Out the door.

'Round the world and back again,
Looking for a cuddly friend.

Not a hog or a frog,
I'm looking for my puppy dog.
Not by his desk,
Not under the table, I wish I could find him,
I wish, I wish.

'Round the world and back again
Looking for a cuddly friend.

Not a calf or a giraffe,
I'm looking for my lizard named Raph.
He's not on the windowsill,
He's not behind the lamp
He's sitting on my cousin, Will.

'Round the world and back again,
Looking for a cuddly friend.

Not a fishy or a birdie,
I'm just looking for my fluffy bunny.
She's not under the stool,
She's not on the couch,
I'm a fool.

I look under the blanket,
And rabbit and puppy pop out!

Kristen Lauren Seese
Age: 9

THE CHILD

I see the staring six year old,
   shivering in the freezing bitter cold.
And yet, the people pass her by,
   staring at her, watching her cry.
Deep down inside me, it makes me feel very sad,
   to know that that child has been treated oh so bad.
I put on my snowsuit, my boots, and my hat,
   and I went to tell that child that her life was all of that.
Then that child looked up at me,
   with a smile upon her face,
   she reminded me of a beautiful white dove,
   full of wonderful grace.
So I took the little girl home with me,
   and she and I became a little family.
And through and through, as the days passed by,
   the child danced, and played, but not once did she cry.
I am very, very proud that I helped that six year old,
   because she would be very unhappy,
   and would not ever be bold.

Teka Rogers
Age: 11

There once was a monster named Brute
Whose face was really a beaut
And his girl Mrs. Godzilla
Made everybody ill-a
Compared to her, Brute was cute.

Josh Darlington
Age: 12

ALIEN

I know of an alien now dead,
Who always ate Mexican bread.
    He got caught by a rock,
And laid there 'round the clock,
    So now he has a flat head.

Danny Lehner
Age: 11

BROWN BREAD

There once was a boy from the dead,
Who liked to eat brown bread.
He went to bed,
And lost his head,
And never ate bread again.

Erik Vogtmann

TOO MUCH LOVE, TOO LITTLE TRUST

The years weighed down my love for him.
The heart began to fade.
Why did he leave?
Was it because of me?
A little girl wanting an older man.
How does this seem?
He ignored my presence.
That was unbearable to me.
Tears I wept for him and now he has vanished from me.
My heart was utterly broken,
for he was a part of me.
He ruled my life into the never-ending eternity.
Such emotions fled through me.
Lust, love, anger, and sorrow.
Why waste so much on this darling man?
He's like all the rest,
but to me, he is the best.
Why is he so loved by me?
His looks? His charm?
What irresistible urge comes over me.
For many years,
I adored him and my eyes grew wide filled with desire.
Was I too loving, too caring?
Has this man ever felt what
I feel now at this moment in time?
Describing my feelings is too revealing.
Why did I fall in love with him?

Shall I someday win his love and affection?
My dreams unraveled before me, cursed and crushed.
All I ever wanted was the only man for me.
Figures, he must not be for me.

D. Rader

FULL MOON

I saw the pretty bright blue sky
The pure red birds as they flew by
Never too late to see it again
Maybe someday in my heart my friend
I'll be back soon
Before I see a full moon

Elisha Lee Corbin
Age: 11

There were little turtles down in the sand.
All of a sudden they burst to the land.
They ran so fast.
They just saw a sea gull capture one little guy.
That little guy whacked his eye.
A big fat iguana ate one little guy.
A little guy bit his toes,
He also bit up an elephant's nose.

David Losh
Age: 11

NUTS

Nuts, nuts,
I'm nuts about nuts, almond, pistachio,
I don't make a fuss, nuts, nuts,
I'm nuts about nuts!
You can make nut huts with nuts, nuts, nuts,
I'm nuts about nuts!

Kasey Kamp
Age: 9

I HAVE A FRIEND

I have a friend.
I have a friend.
She's so kind
So kind I say.
She is kind every day.
We never fight.
We always play.
And that is why
We are friends every day.

Abigail Powell
Age: 8

LEAVES

Leaves have so many colors.
Yellow, orange, red, green and brown.
Leaves are so beautiful.
They dance and prance
In the sky all day.
They fly as if they were birds,
Flying to the south.
Watch them slide, turn and wiggle.
But when they drop on the ground,
You have to watch more.
Leaves, leaves what would I do without you?

Kelsey Lynett
Age: 9

ALL ABOUT BEARS!

All about bears.
Bears like to sleep through the winter.
Bears shuffle through a dry autumn meadow
In a National Park.
Day after day, the bears eat and store their food
Before the winter.
When winter gets here,
The bear finds a place to hibernate.
The bear sleeps and sleeps into spring.

Nathaniel Leon Fitch
Age: 10

DAVID JUSTICE

David Justice is so good
He hit a ball out of the neighborhood
It went so far it hit a car
And bounced into a little kid's yard

Deven Legg
Age: 9

THANKSGIVING

Thanksgiving is wonderful,
It is so beautiful.
The trees are bare,
The weather isn't fair.
The meal is so bountiful.

Heather Hill

THE CROSS-COUNTRY RACE

Hundreds of runners huddle by a thick,
white starting line.
You stretch every muscle in your body, run in place,
and jog a few feet and back to loosen up.
It's now time and all the runners line up,
forming a long row of feet like a mile long centipede.
It becomes quiet.
There are three whistles, a pause, one last whistle,
then the gun sounds; echoing across the field.
Your adrenaline starts pumping.
Some speed ahead, some fall behind.
The pressure causes a thunderstorm in your stomach.
After the first mile,
some are a distant twenty feet ahead.
You catch up and pass a few
with your calves starting to burn.
The second mile goes by
and your lungs are like a balloon ready to pop
but you need to give this last mile your all.
Your legs tighten to rocks
as you pass five more runners.
You see the end with your dry, bloodshot eyes.
Pushing it to your limit,
your lungs are ready to explode.
You cross the line, you are there -- it is over.
Body dripping with sweat, you guzzle some water,
lay back in the grass and fall asleep.

Aaron Joles
Age: 16

WOODLAND SCHOOL

There was a class at Woodland School,
Who was really, really cool.
When they went on a trip,
They came back sick.
And would never follow the rule.

Kamila Jaroniec
Age: 8

COOL POOL

I have a pool,
That is cool.
It will never last,
But it is fast.
I like swimming with a fool.

Emily Knapp

MORNING'S ANTICIPATION

The early morning dawn's crisp and cool.
The layer of fog so thick wraps around you
like a blanket of wool.
From the barn comes a quiet rustling of fresh straw.
It's the pregnant nut brown mare with black mane
and tail in her stall.
She's up pacing nervously with anticipation.
The time is now say her eyes sparkling with elation.
For a mother can tell things that others cannot.
First comes the front legs and head,
so dainty and small.
Next comes the body then back legs,
spindle-like and tall.
It's a girl, a filly, with coat of cinnamon and snow-white.
Get up urges mother,
her soft nicker holding a gentle might.
She helps her daughter up
with a loving nudge from her nose.
The filly then stumbles up onto her legs in a shaky,
uncertain pose.
Slowly and carefully she makes her way to her mother
to get something to drink.
Her mother turns to look at her,
the most beautiful thing, she thinks.

Jennifer Jilling
Age: 16

GOD SAVES THOSE WHO CRY OUT

It was a scorching hot day
when the girl walked out of the house
that was filled with horror.
The hate filled the streets of Harlem
that late autumn afternoon.
She walked across the abandoned streets
down four blocks until she came to a deserted lot.
She fell to her knees onto the hot asphalt
as her heart filled with intense anger
from the overwhelming hurt that overflowed her insides.
She looked up to the white heavens above
and prayed to her God to lift her up to the skies above.
God answered and said "Stand up my precious child
Spread your arms as wings and begin to soar,
If you fall I will help you."
The girl got up spread her arms as wings
and began to soar.
The next day the girl was back to all the hatred.
She walked to her deserted lot again
and laid upon the asphalt and cried to God.
"Please God take me to your world of honor and glory.
It must be better than this."
God looked at her lifeless, motionless body and said,
"My precious one I can't bear to see you like this,
you tried ot spread your wings and soar,
but you couldn't.
I still love you. Fall asleep and dream of my Heaven.
When you see it spread your wings and fly."

She did as she was told.
God lifted her up and the skies opened
and the whole world could see her.
They saw all the peace and love that surrounded
this kingdom so far away, yet so near.
From that day forward Harlem was no longer known
as the town of horror and hatefulness.

Karen D. Madden

HOW THE DEER PRANCE

How the deer prance!
It looks like the deer dance
as they prance in the meadows
and at night you can see their shadows
But if they were to see your shadows
they would sense the smell of danger
and they would run like the wind

Shanon Goodrich
Age: 11

FIVE LITTLE GERBILS

Five little gerbils
Feed from their mother
The fattest one
Like no other.

Five little gerbils
Colored black and brown
Two little eyes
By their crown.

Five little gerbils
Their tongues so pink
But boy, oh boy,
Do they stink.

Five little gerbils
Their smiles so bright
A cat jumps up
That's quite a fright.

Kehla Denee Carr
Age: 11

MY BEST FRIEND

Me and my best friend
are very good together.
When we play in the snow
we have hot cocoa.

Cara Steffy
Age: 9

READING

Reading feeds my brain,
Oh how it loves to read!
It fills me with knowledge,
And a need to read more more more!

Amy Striff

EXPLORING THE OCEAN

One nestling took a testing in the ocean.
He went through the sparkling waves
And went through the coves.
And he made a wish for colorful fish.
He saw the underwater plants
And his pants almost fell down.
The hatch had another match with another fish.

Stephanie Orlando
Age: 10

THE MAN WHO WAS COOL

There was a man who was cool.
And when he was cool,
He got so mad that he got blue,
And he knew,
That he got fooled by a mule.

Elliot Weiner

FALL

F un to run around.
A nxious to jump in the leaves.
L istening to the breath of the wind.
L eaves falling off the trees.

Geoff Domchick
Age: 10

A MOUSE

There was a mouse,
Who lives in a house.
She had a class,
And her class was outside in the grass.
She always wore a blouse.

Sara Whitlinger

E ating, edible, exceptional
A nswering phones
S picy sandwiches
T asting, tany

O rdering, operating
F easting, festival

C hef's salad, coming to you
H ealthy, hungry
I nternational pizza
C raving, crusty, cheesy, cut perfectly
A wesome, any flavor
G arden pizza or salad
O pen 'til eleven o'clock p.m.

P izza, pick up, party, pepperoni
I t smells delightful
Z esty, zing
Z ip, zooms right to you!!
A ny kind, anywhere

Kelsey Evans
Age: 9

THANKSGIVING

Thank you for my eyes,
that allow me to see,
all those wonderful things,
that you've put around me.

Thank you for my ears,
that allow me to hear,
all those wonderful things,
that you whisper in my ear.

Thank you for my spirit, heart, and soul,
so that I will always know,
that you will be with me,
wherever I go.

Taylor Ashley Rose
Age: 10

EAGLE

Eagle
powerful bird
loves to eat great big trout
gliding with pride over the land
Great bird

Clinton Moyers
Age: 11

GOOD-BYE SUMMER

Good-bye sports,
Good-bye shorts.
Good-bye bikes,
No more hikes.

Why does it always go?
Now I'm stuck here in the snow.
But, stay here,
Because there is always next year!

Kosta Elefter
Age: 9

FUN DAY

Once upon a time
We tried to make a rhyme
It wasn't very easy
So we went to play Parcheesi
But soon that got boring
And I heard Mommy snoring
So I woke her with a shake
And baked her a little cake
And when we thought of all that fun
We realized our poem was done

Shannon L. Farrell
Age: 9

NATURE

Nature has beauty
With the sun shining with love
And all the trees growing above.
When you open your door,
You might hear the ocean roar.
As you hear the wind howl,
You might hear the hoot of an owl.

The grass is green
And the river that flows
All the time, as it rains and snows.
Look at the beautiful sky,
And watch the birds go as they fly by.

With creatures on land,
And fish in the sea
Nature fills you with majesty.

From the stars in the sky,
To the plants underground
You can see nature all around.
Nature is all around the earth,
So now you know how much nature is worth!!

Stephanie Klein
Age: 9

Cats
fluffy, cuddly,
loving, caring, obeying
rubbing fur against skin
Feline

Kristin Brustoski
Age: 10

I BROKE IT

I broke my brother's jet
He was very upset
He chased me down the hall
And called me a goofball
I wanted to go so I said good-bye
But first he gave me a black eye

Alyssa Nischt

DEATH

What we think seems to fear,
day-by-day we are one step near,
every second we are dying,
our thoughts are clear.
People think and say why
When it happens its results to cry.
But death to me is just away,
of being packed in the clay.
What we see is not what happens,
the good Lord points at his mappings
and off it goes to the sky,
or if you're bad, in Hell you'll die.

Theresa Hunter
Age: 13

THANKSGIVING DAY

Thanksgiving day is a time for sharing
Good food, family, and friends
When everybody is caring
I hope this day never ends

There is a lot of happiness here
We have much to be thankful for
I hope that I made this clear
Because next year we'll be back for more

Danny Simon
Age: 9

HARD QUESTIONS

A hard question...
What do I want to be?
A druggie, or someone that wants to be free,
That's all determined by me.

Another hard question...
Should I live or should I die?
Being alive's horrible 'cause I hate life.
Being dead's the best 'cause in Hell's
the place I should be.
That's all determined by me.

One more hard question...
Can I honestly say I'm not in
a gang?
Yes, but a gang's the best place for
someone like me.

These questions can be answered
by one person,
That's me.
This stuff is determined what I want to do or be.

Andrea Sarvey
Age: 13

A SPECIAL SOMEONE

There was a special
person, but now
he's gone.
In my heart he'll
always carry on.
I have the best of
memories of him
with me.
He was always there
with a helping hand,
ready to guide me along.
Understanding and caring
is what you would
call my father.
The man who did
it all for me.
The man who
is the
world to me.

Rose Yanno
Age: 14

A LOVELY DAY WILL MAKE ME SMILE

A lovely day can make me smile
And keep me happy for a while.
But nothing feels as good and true
As sharing a life with people like you.
Once I was feeling bad then,
I thought I'd never smile again.
A rainy day makes me sad,
When there's a rainy day I won't be glad.
A rainy day won't make me smile
Not even for a little while.
But when there's sun I'll go and play,
Because it'll be a sunny day.
I should have known you all would be
Such perfect, helpful friends to me.
I thank you for all and like you so
I'm happier than you'll ever know!

Jasmine Lattice Webster
Age: 9

CHESS

C astling my king when it's in check.
H a ha ha's and boohoo boohoo's.
E xecuting my enemy's queen.
S aving my castle.
S acrificing my knight.

Abbaad Haider
Age: 9

SUMMER

Summer stays way too short.
I hate to see it go.
It's fun to play every day.
Outside in the sun, not snow.

I wish summer could last forever.
Well, maybe if I tried,
I could see summer in my dreams
And laugh instead of cry.

Jennah Siskovic
Age: 8

OHIO

Ohio is pretty, Ohio is sweet,
Ohio is like dancing, as you tap to the beat.
Look at the cardinal as it flies by,
Watch it closely, look it right in the eye.
Look at the flowers all bright pink and red,
It sometimes makes you feel like
You are nowhere else instead.
Some people don't like it in Ohio,
That is very, very true,
But I hope it's no one else, especially not you.

Keli Ann Shabella
Age: 9

STUBBORN TEETH

I still have all my baby teeth,
I push them very hard, wait!
I think one's loose!
No, just my finger seemed to make it move.
In five months it's my birthday!
So far I've lost five teeth;
Two dollars for each one.

Five months later it's my birthday!
Five more teeth I've lost!
Three dollars for every one.
It didn't hurt at all;
Three of them I pulled,
One the dentist pulled, two of them fell out.
When I ate an apple,
The other ones I wiggled out!

I've lost ten teeth.
I don't have stubborn teeth anymore,
Hey, I think one's loose!
Yeah! Two of them!

Margaret Matavich
Age: 8

CHOCOLATE

Chocolate,
Chocolate
Is so sweet
When I bite it
It makes me
Feel so neat!
I think about it
All the time.
It's always
On my mind.
I love it!
I can't wait
To eat it!
It's my very
Favorite treat!

Courtney Stein
Age: 9

FLY

Fly, fly
Annoying me
Buzzing 'round and 'round.
If he keeps annoying me,
I'll swat him to the ground!

Daniel Ross
Age: 9

BASEBALL

When the pitcher
Throws the ball
I don't feel
My feet at all!
It was the
Bottom of the ninth
Runner on third,
Tie game,
Two outs.
I was up to bat,
Infielders moved in...
I read the pitch
Hoping to get a base hit...
I swung...
It was slammed
To deep center field...
Way back,
Way back,
It was...
Gone!
We were the champions!

Nathan Brode
Age: 8

BASEBALL

Three bases
One home plate
A batter
A pitcher
The ball is hit!
It's going...
It's going...
IT'S GONE!
The runner
Speeds around first
Flies around second
Zooms around third...
HOME RUN!

Courtney Porter
Age: 8

MY BEST FRIEND

My friend is
Extraordinary!
She's always fun,
Always there for me.
She's helpful.
She's kind.
We share secrets
And giggle a lot!

Suneet Dhillon
Age: 8

WAGON

Yesterday at my friends,
I pushed him in his wagon.
He sat down,
He took the handle,
And I began to push.
He did a sharp turn,
And fell out,
But he was O.K.
I pushed him 'til it got cold,
And then I went home,
And thought about the fun,
I had pushing him in,
His wagon.

Samantha Streb
Age: 9

BEST FRIENDS

I have a lot of friends
Who are really nice to me.
Most important though
Is a friend who
Lets me be myself,
Protects my secrets,
And listens with gentle ears.

Mackenzie Russell
Age: 8

T-SHIRTS

T-shirts can go anywhere
To the movies
To the park
Even in the dark
They can go to see Dominique Moceanu
Even to Kalamazoo
They are all different colors
Green, white, and blue
They look good on everyone even
YOU!

Danielle Pavlansky
Age: 9

MY BUNNY AND ME

My bunny is curious,
Cuddly and cute.
When I am busy,
She sniffs and hops
Around the garage
And discovers something
To nibble and crunch.
I chase her and know...
By the evidence on her toes!

Alan Jarmusch
Age: 9

GLASSES

Last Monday, at my baseball game,
something just wasn't quite the same.
I couldn't seem to hit the ball,
I wasn't any good at all.

So Tuesday, after school I went
to my optician, Dr. Brent.
In the waiting room, I looked around
and a "Highlights" magazine I found.

As I got into a story,
I looked up and saw Miss Maury,
"The doctor is ready to see you, dear."
And my heart began to fill with fear.

I sat in the chair and looked at the chart,
but the letters seemed to blend, not part.
The doctor said, "Read the top line."
So I did, and he said, "Fine."

But then a twist that made me mad,
"Read the last line," and when I had,
the words I dreaded to hear,
"You need glasses, come over here."

I tried them on, and it was a surprise,
I could see clearly with my eyes.

I looked in the mirror; they weren't bad,
"There you go, my happy young lad."

Benjamin Calvert Wagner
Age: 13

MY LITTLE BROTHER

My brother's awful, bad,
Stupid, looney, psycho,
A nightmare, cuckoo.
My brother's nice, kind,
Generous, helpful, loving.
But when he's sweet...
He wants something!

Alex Siegle
Age: 9

ED

There once was a man named Ed,
He had a very big head.
He had red shoe laces,
And he made bookcases.
And he loved to make white bread.

Kaitlin Begley

SHADOWS

The shadows that trail us are the
shadows that became friends.
The shadows went through mistakes
and hardships as well as the
fun and crazy dances on the curbside.
The tune of that dance carried us
through the holding onto one another
as we shed our tears.
Through all this the shadows had
each other.
Like no other shadows there were
three that sometimes went through
feelings of hate, and also neglect,
but through all this the shadows
had each other.
The three shadows were like no others
they always held onto one another.
As the shadows split apart they always
wander together and never die
because they have each other.

Tara Lynn Shevetz
Age: 17

SEASON

Winter began one morning as a cool, chilly,
nippy, emotionless feeling.
Sleeping under the covers like toast in a toaster
I instantly feel the shivery, icy,
frigid air as I jump out of bed.
The icy cold floor stings my barefeet.
Winter has begun.

It was the afternoon of a beautiful spring day.
The lovely afternoon was so delightful
I never wanted it to end.
It was one of a kind.
Spring has begun.

Bright colorful red, orange, yellow leaves
walk through people's lawns.
Pumpkins and cornstalks
become entangled with the leaves.
Cool, nippy, crisp nights tell me fall has begun.

Baking under the hot sun
I felt a sense of sweltering heat.
Skin sizzling, blistering, and scorching.
Feeling like fire ants crawling on me.
Oh my! Summer has begun.

Christine Miller
Age: 11

MY FRIEND

To me, my friend is like a sister.
She is always there for me,
Always ready to talk about anything.
She is always so caring,
         so loving,
         so understanding,
And everything else a friend,
Or sister would be.
She is very dear to me.

If she were ever to die,
Part of me would die with her;
But part of her would stay alive in me.

Melanie Beil
Age: 13

OCTOBER

October is cold
It may snow then
October is neat

Samantha Brandon
Age: 8

COLORLESS WORLD

Sitting in class,
My mind began to
wonder far away.
What would it be
like in a colorless world,
where nothing had color,
and everything was gray
and drab?
Nothing had color,
and everything
and everybody was the same.
As I sat there
wondering about the
colorless world, I tried
to imagine what the
world would be like cold,
dark and gray.
What would the
world look like without color?
Would it be the
same over and over and over?
Or would it be
boring jut the same?

Amanda Yeager
Age: 13

SUN

Let the sun light your lamp;
let her give you the warmth of fire.
Let her shed the night away,
And start a brand-new day.

See her cry tears of raindrops.
See her smile the colors of the rainbow.
See her dance when she shines.
See her shiver when it snows.

She will always give us heat.
She will always give us light.
She will always give us day.
She will always give us night.

Angela Bortmas
Age: 12

CONFUSION

Sometimes when you feel down,
or you're left hanging around.
You think it's not worth living for,
and you just wanna walk out the door.
Confusion can be subtle or even incomplete,
it will leave you hanging off the edge of your seat.

Tiffany Marie TurnBull
Age: 13

WOLF TALK

Soon I saw where another wolf
had left the island to trot out on the lake.
Its tracks merged with the others where
the wolves had come nose-to-nose,
likely sniffing and muzzling each other.
They continued north together, one behind the other,
their paws of motion fading into the moonlight....

But where were the wolves now?
Did they know I was there?
Were their bodies camouflaged
among shadows of tree trunks?
Was that my heartbeat I heard
or the shuffling of wolf paws on snow?

Lisa Elizabeth Hull
Age: 12

SPRING

Spring is warm weather,
With beautiful flowers all around.
And butterflies flying everywhere.
Children play morning 'til night,
As parents sit and relax.
Say bye to the spring weather,
As the hot summer weather comes.

Christine Coontz
Age: 11

THANK YOU

The torture and the taunts,
The insults and the jokes,
The names and the actions,
were all part of my life.
Every day I would walk through the halls,
and people would snicker behind my back,
"Oh, isn't she ugly?"
I'd NEVER talk to her!"
"Watch out or she'll fall on you!"
they would tease me about my weight,
and make fun of me, as if I didn't even exist,
as if I were some toy of theirs to play with,
as if I had absolutely no emotions at all.
But you never did,
you stuck up for me,
you stood between me and them,
and defended me, you protected me.
You were my one and only true friend,
the only one that cared,
and I'm sorry,
I'm so sorry.
I wasn't there for you,
I let you down,
down too far to bring back up.
You needed me and I was nowhere to be found.
I should have been with you
when they took you and beat you
all because you were my friend.
I should have been there
when they buried you in trash
and threw rocks at you,
because you stood up for me,

because you weren't a coward,
because you were brave.
I need you to forgive me,
and I need you to understand,
that I'm sorry.
I can't forgive myself,
but I hope you can.
When I see you in Heaven,
I hope that then,
I can stand up for you and be there,
like I should have been.
All I can say now is thank you.
Thank you for being you,
and not siding with the cruel, inhuman
classmates that killed you,
then went to see a movie.
Thank you for being kind,
generous and caring.
Thank you.
Thank you.

Ashley Miller
Age: 12

The sidewalk is hot
From the beating of the sun
On a summer's day

Eric Prior
Age: 13

THE CROCHETING OF SNOWFLAKES

An old lady lives among the l o u d
c   s

  She
     S
      i
       t
        s
          in her rocking chair

crocheting snowflakes
  telling stories to the children
      of the WIND,

  She
     s
      i
       t
        s
          in her chair and
  rocks b
        a
         c
          k
           and forth
with a SQueak of delight
crocheting the patterns and
  watching them F
           A
            L
             L...

a blanket of white for the
Sleeping earth

Jessica Ashdown
Age: 13

FALL'S COLORFUL RAIN

the ornate trees of f   sway in the cool
                    a
                    l
                    l
        cool breeze leaves f
                            a
                            l
                            l
                            i
                            n
                            g
like a raiN not of water but of FirE
crunching UnDeR your Feet...the LeAveS
wither and DIE

Jacob Massacci
Age: 13

FRED AND HIS FRUITS

Fred ate some juicy fruits last night.
He was amazed when he took a bite.
He then saw a worm,
That started to squirm.
So he went outside to fly his kite.

Autumn Hoffstetter
Age: 13

SNOW

When the snow begins to fall,
it falls in little droplets,
all with six perfect points,
cold, pale, and silent,
in darkness or in light.
Snow is like a graceful dancer,
falling to the ground,
wondering if they'll ever,
ever get up again.
Snow can be so peaceful,
then the next minute,
being thrown back and forth,
through little children's hands.
Snow is always changing,
it will never be the same.

Julie M. Bresnahan
Age: 12

DREAMS ARE...

Dreams are little scenes,
That play inside ones head.
They may be little hopes,
That you dream when you're in bed.

Dreams bring all happiness,
When you think of something glad.
They'll bring you hopes of what you'll be,
Instead of making you mad.

Dreams can be scary,
For instance nightmares.
That give little children,
A frightening little scare.

So dream a little dream,
That makes you really happy.
You'll dream of a nightmare,
If you make Mom real snappy.

Bonnie J. Ward
Age: 13

AIRPLANES

Airplanes can fly very high,
To reach out and touch the sky.
From fighter to war or for just plain fun,
It doesn't look as one may ever reach the sun.
In the 1600's all they could do was run,
Many succeeded but many would wreck.
They come right in and hit the deck,
From death to a scratch from a signal to a wreck.
You can see the clouds across the sky.
Ready to take off for another flight,
And reach a fleet maybe another height.
You may live to tell or you may die.

Nate Harnett
Age: 12

IT WAS MY BIRTHDAY PARTY

It was my birthday party.
I couldn't wait to see
All the wonderful presents,
They were all for me.
They were big and small,
Bags and all,
Square and circle,
Pink and purple.
They were all for me!

Alison Wynne
Age: 10

Roshey
clumsy, wacky
playing, chasing, running
wanting to explore things
Fuzzball

Pamela Marie Miller
Age: 9

THE WONDERFUL ONE

He lives
In the clouds.
No one
Has seen Him.
He is bright
And beautiful.
He paints pictures
In the sky.
At night the moon
Is his fingernail.
God is who
I'm talking about
And all His
Angel friends.
I love Him.
I hope you do too.
He loves me
And He loves you.

Signe Knutson
Age: 9

SCOOBY--DOO

He was born on the Fourth of July...
  and was one special guy!
A little puff of white and gray;
  he came home with us to stay.
He was with us 'til he was almost seventeen,
  and was a very big part of our family team.

Four children called him pet,
  and he was the best...on this you could bet!
Playmate, guard, and friend,
  on him you could always depend.
He came running at the clap of two hands,
  we always thought he'd be part of our plan.

As time went on...he walked so slow,
  and no longer cared about hiding in the snow.
On sunny days, he slept a lot...
  instead of chasing a ball about.
The day came when we had to part,
  but he'll always be in our hearts.

The house now is plain,
  on the wall...there hangs no dog chain.
I miss his bark...
  and the walks in the park.
His eyes so bright...
  his fur soft...gray, tan, and white.

The jingle of his collar tags,
  his curled, fluffy tail wag!
His cold, wet nose...
  nudging the family that he chose.

His ears perked straight up!
  he was a very loveable pup!!
Yes... we'll always remember you...
  we'll miss you.... SCOOBY--DOO!!!

Shaun Michael Dunmire
Age: 10

THE WEEPING WILLOW

In a lonely abandoned field,
Where only green grass will grow,
I sit in the shade of my good friend,
The Weeping Willow.

I write stories there night and day,
Sometimes I come with nothing to say,
When I'm gone, his leaves begin to sway,
Teardrops fall he begins to say,

Come back, come back, and visit me.
For you are my only true friend.
Without you, I shall cry and sob with no end.
I'm looking,
Looking up to my name,
My leaves are hanging low,
But that is why I must be sorrowfully called,
The Weeping Willow.

Stephanie Lynn Bloomquist
Age: 13

THANKSGIVING DAY

Oh, Dear Lord, to you I pray,
Thank you for Thanksgiving day.
Please help me to follow your way,
With each and every passing day.
Help me see what you want me to see,
Help me be what you want me to be.
Help me see in all the others,
That they are my sisters and brothers.
Guide my steps each and every day,
Help me do things in a Christian way.
Thank you Dear Lord for helping me be,
All of the things you want me to be.

Jason Kyle Debelyak
Age: 11

BASEBALL

When I am out on the field I look so thrilled
and I see a lot of batters.
When they hit it so far,
it hits a car and shatters.
When I am up to bat,
I hit a kid named Matt,
and he goes down on the ground
And I go running around.
As I am heading home, I score one more,
to make it one to four!

Robert Mistovich
Age: 11

THE BOG DOG

There once was a dog,
Who lived in a bog.
His light was dim,
And he couldn't swim.
So then he got lost in the fog.

Jessica Poiner

AN ARTIFICIAL TREE

Gone are the years we pick out a tree,
Now we get one in a box marked buy one get one free.
No more discussions about the width or the height,
Now the sales clerk asks us green or white.
Christmas used to be the best time of the year,
Now I catch myself wiping away a tear.
Remembering the fun we had
In the field kicking a beehive,
Now we have to pay $19.95.
So there it stands, my artificial tree,
With the presents around it waiting for me.
But don't you worry, don't you fret,
I guess I don't have any regrets;
For it doesn't matter what the tree is worth,
All that matters is the day of our Savior's birth.

Dana Palazzo
Age: 10

MY GERBILS

My fuzzy, black gerbils are real pest.
They keep me up all night and I don't get any rest.
They chewed through their cage and ate up their dish.
Sometimes I think I'd rather have a fish.
When they run on their wheel it squeaks all night
And when we try to feed them they start to bite.
If I can't have a real pet I guess they'll do
But if I ever get a cat I'll know who to feed them too.

Bethany Sauline
Age: 10

WINTER

Winter is when the ground turns white,
And you can have a snowball fight.
Dress up as warm as you can,
Before you go out and build a snowman.
Give him a carrot for a nose,
Put him in a silly pose.
Go sledding with a friend.

Julia George
Age: 10

BOWLING

Bowling is a nice sport to play,
I bowl on a team every Saturday.

I have a teammate named Mike,
Who almost always gets a strike.

When my ball hits the floor,
My dad is keeping score.

If my ball goes in the gutter,
It makes me want to mutter.

I always want to knock down the most pins,
Because whoever gets the most points wins.

Brian Matthew Stevens
Age: 10

JESUS

Jesus is as special as he can be,
He knows your deepest thoughts,
And makes you feel happy,
And when you're feeling sad,
Remember that you're the best,
And will always be together in unity.

Ashley Ruozzo
Age: 10

THE WEEPING SANTA

Winter night and candlelight,
All the children's faces are bright,
But no one knows of the weeping Santa woes,
For children are all aglow,
As they wait for St. Nicholas who is sure to show,
But all have forgotten except Santa who mourns,
Because he knows no one remembers
The day Christ was born.

Samantha Gigax
Age: 10

SUMMER EVENING

Darkness is creeping
Air so damp,
Dew covers the ground,
The moon like a lamp.
Dew covers the ground
No movement is made,
The gentle breeze flows
The sun starts to fade.

Carrie Hart
Age: 12

THE STRIKE OUT

It is strike two on the batter,
Is he going to swing and miss?

He looks at the pitcher,
And anticipates the next pitch.

The batter swings,
And the umpire says to thee,
It is a swing and a miss,
It is strike three!

Andrew Straub
Age: 11

DOG

The dog, king of the canines
The dog that chases cats
The dog that is my pet
The dog that hates bats

The dog that is so nice
The dog that hates ice
The dog that has a great mood
The dog that likes dog food

Trevor Adam Rapp
Age: 9

MORNING AT MY WINDOW

Blue lake winking from the morning sun
The damp flowers drip from the morning dew
Birds are chirping ducks are quacking
Trees and grass grow in the morning
My dog barks happily as he waits for his morning meal
He leaves his little pawprints in the wet grass
Bright blue sky white fluffy clouds
Bright yellow sun burns the dew
As the new day arrives

Todd Creed

MY BEST FRIEND

My best friend doesn't sit by me in school,
But to love me forever is her number one rule.
She can't talk to me with words but she knows what
To do when I have a bad day or I am feeling blue.
Our friendship is forever our love is too.
My best friend is my dog,
Brave, loyal and true.

Joseph Corpa
Age: 10

THANKSGIVING

We're so sick of dry beef jerky,
Let's have some guests and roast a turkey.

Fix it with beans, bread, and corn on the cob,
We'll share it with a guy named Bob.

Michael Henry DeMart
Age: 11

CHRISTMAS EVE!!

There's a hint of magic in the air
People rushing everywhere.
Children's bright smiles light up the night
Like a Christmas tree's bright lights.
Gifts are wrapped under the tree
Soon children will awake happy as can be.

Michelle High
Age: 10

RAINBOW

A beautiful, beautiful rainbow,
So colorful and bright.
Oh, how I love that rainbow,
Especially, if I could see it at night!

Ashtan Williams
Age: 9

JIM

My friend, Jim,
He fits in size "slim."
He got blown really high,
Way up to the sky.
But nobody believes it was him.

Nicholas Divjak
Age: 10

FRIGHT!

Fright would not make you fly a kite!
Let me take you to a place where fright is the case.
Do you dare to enter the night.
No, no, don't there is too much fright.
But if you dare to step into the night you
Will no longer have fright.
It will be darker than the night!

Kevin Beebe
Age: 13

CHARLIE

Charlie is my
Kindergarten brother
I teach him his ABC's
And his one, two, threes
He wears leg braces
And sometimes falls
But when we wrestle
He wins it all!

J. Alexander Cryder
Age: 8

WHAT MY DOG LOOKS LIKE

My dog has gray hair,
She has a pink tongue.
My dog has a short tail,
She has eyes that look like chocolate.
My dog has a black nose,
That looks like a button.
She has ears that are floppy
My dog looks like a blanket.

Alex Swick
Age: 9

MY TEACHER

My teacher is so nice and kind,
She stimulates my mind.
Why is she so nice?
Why do people look for mice?
My favorite subject is math,
(My teacher teaches it so nice!!)
My teacher is so nice and kind,
She stimulates my mind!

Catherine R. Colitre
Age: 8

WHY?

Why does my sister take after her own kind?
Why is she so pale in the spine?
Why are her legs so big, and her head as small as a pea?
Oh please tell me why please, please, please.
Why does she always fall on her knees?
Why does she always kick and punch so hard?
If you can answer these questions
I'll give you a million dollars,
But I'm afraid they can't be answered.
Because her history tells
That she used to live on the planet Y.

Tiffany Watson
Age: 11

HATCHLINGS POINT OF VIEW

Please don't let me die
By the flying things in the sky.
I'm getting tired now.
I can't stop or else I'll probably die.
Now I'm in the blue water.
I see colorful fish, sponges, and plants.
There are still more dangers ahead.

Nick Henthorn
Age: 12

YOU'RE MY EXAMPLE

In a cruel and thoughtless world
Where our views are often dim,
The world would be a better place
If there were more like him.

If our eye's could only see
Those who can't stand alone,
Those who are too weak
To pass life on their own.

A young girl lay sick and weak
Confined to a hospital bed.
He could have stayed with his friends,
But he went to her instead.

If we could see those people,
Whose lives are hard to endure.
If we could only give some time
Like he had done for her.

If only people turned around
And tried a brand-new start.
Gave up a little, just like him,
And showed a kinder heart.

I have seen
The thoughtful things you do.

You are my example, I'll follow God
And live the same as you.

Mary Teske
Age: 13

Baseball
exciting, fast
pitching, hitting, running
rough, exciting, catching game
Babe Ruth

Greg Garcia

THE CAT SAT ON A MAT

Once a very fluffy cat
sat on a small red and blue mat.
Then he got off to sit on the floor
to see if he could open the door.
Then he got the door open
but then he tripped on a red and blue pen.
Then he wrote with the pen
but then he fell into a den.
Then he went into a teepee
so he could watch a lot of TV.
Then he went back to the mat
so he could be a fluffy cat.

Melissa Penkava
Age: 8

J ump
A ll
M all
I love you

Jami Gangwer
Age: 6

February 23rd
presents, celebration
exciting, eating, festivity
enjoying, eager, party, pride
My birthday

Jeffrey Lee
Age: 9

D ownright loyal.
O utstandingly cute.
G eniusly smart.
S illy and humorous.

John Rausch

FROGS

Fat frogs frolic from
Fat lily pads for
Fifteen minutes.

Jacob B. Ross
Age: 11

FEELINGS

I am a boy who gets made fun of a lot.
And when I do I get hurt.
Sometimes I feel like
I could beat the tar out of the person.
But I always keep my cool.

Matthew Ward

CHRISTMAS

I like Christmas because I like being with my family,
And the food and playing games with my family,
And we have the games I like.

Brian Nixdorf
Age: 9

SYLVESTER

Sylvester flies 'round and 'round
Trying to catch Tweety.
He squirms, he swirms, twists and turns
And finally learns?
He can't catch Tweety!

Andy Minno
Age: 9

The fish who gets his fin in a can
May never get it out ever again
The otter saves him
The serpent eats him
And all is well for the serpent

Kyle Fulton
Age: 9

SWEET ROSE

Sweet rose that covers the land,
Sweet rose that cheers us up,
Sweet rose that fills our lives,
Sweet rose that falls in love,
Sweet rose that fills the room,
Sweet rose that gives us joy,
Sweet rose that we give,
Sweet rose that I give to you.

Daniel Jones
Age: 9

SNOW

Snow on the rooftops
It's whirling all around me
Snow is beautiful.

Holly Calvelli
Age: 9

I like to eat snow.
I like to throw the snowballs.
People make snowmen.

Andrew Burnett
Age: 12

MOONLIGHT LOVE

As the dark moonlight reflected off the sea,
I saw her standing above.
There could be no soul more beautiful than she,
Pouring forth all heaven's love.
Shining brightly this winged seraph drew near to me.
I had felt peace like a dove.

She was at peace and I was at peace also.
The sea with heaven's pure love,
She with flowing white dress blowing in the soft breeze,
Her name was Sara LaKove.
This was a moment I wanted to seize,
I had fallen in love.

Johnny Woodford
Age: 13

MY TRUCK

I love my truck,
So does my Dad.
I have a 350 motor in my truck.
It's very nifty,
It's very gnarly,
Just like a Harley.

Andrew S. Hickman
Age: 9